THE BEATLES FOR TWO

Arrangements by Mark Phillips

Cover photo: CBS Photo Archive via Getty Images

ISBN 978-1-5400-4818-9

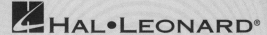

Visit Hal Leonard Online at
www.halleonard.com

Contact us:
Hal Leonard
7777 West Bluemound Road
Milwaukee, WI 53213
Email: info@halleonard.com

In Europe, contact:
Hal Leonard Europe Limited
42 Wigmore Street
Marylebone, London, W1U 2RN
Email: info@halleonardeurope.com

In Australia, contact:
Hal Leonard Australia Pty. Ltd.
4 Lentara Court
Cheltenham, Victoria, 3192 Australia
Email: info@halleonard.com.au

ALL MY LOVING

VIOLINS

Words and Music by JOHN LENNON
and PAUL McCARTNEY

ALL YOU NEED IS LOVE

VIOLINS

Words and Music by JOHN LENNON
and PAUL McCARTNEY

AND I LOVE HER

VIOLINS

Words and Music by JOHN LENNON
and PAUL McCARTNEY

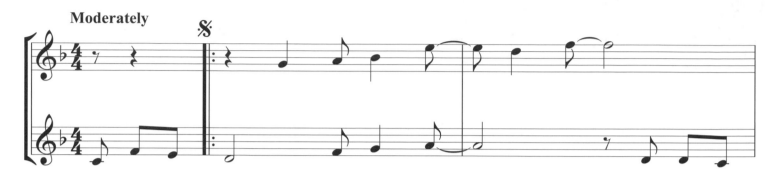

ELEANOR RIGBY

VIOLINS

Words and Music by JOHN LENNON
and PAUL McCARTNEY

Moderately fast

THE FOOL ON THE HILL

VIOLINS

Words and Music by JOHN LENNON
and PAUL McCARTNEY

Moderately slow, in 2

GOLDEN SLUMBERS

VIOLINS

Words and Music by JOHN LENNON
and PAUL McCARTNEY

Moderately slow

HERE COMES THE SUN

VIOLINS

Words and Music by
GEORGE HARRISON

Moderately fast

HERE, THERE AND EVERYWHERE

VIOLINS

Words and Music by JOHN LENNON
and PAUL McCARTNEY

HEY JUDE

VIOLINS

Words and Music by JOHN LENNON
and PAUL McCARTNEY

I SAW HER STANDING THERE

Violins

Words and Music by JOHN LENNON
and PAUL McCARTNEY

I WANT TO HOLD YOUR HAND

VIOLINS

Words and Music by JOHN LENNON
and PAUL McCARTNEY

I WILL

VIOLINS

Words and Music by JOHN LENNON
and PAUL McCARTNEY

LET IT BE

VIOLINS

Words and Music by JOHN LENNON
and PAUL McCARTNEY

THE LONG AND WINDING ROAD

VIOLINS

Words and Music by JOHN LENNON
and PAUL McCARTNEY

Moderately slow

MICHELLE

VIOLINS

Words and Music by JOHN LENNON
and PAUL McCARTNEY

Moderately slow, in 2

NORWEGIAN WOOD

(This Bird Has Flown)

VIOLINS

Words and Music by JOHN LENNON
and PAUL McCARTNEY

OB-LA-DI, OB-LA-DA

VIOLINS

Words and Music by JOHN LENNON
and PAUL McCARTNEY

PENNY LANE

VIOLINS

Words and Music by JOHN LENNON
and PAUL McCARTNEY

SHE LOVES YOU

VIOLINS

Words and Music by JOHN LENNON
and PAUL McCARTNEY

SOMETHING

VIOLINS

Words and Music by
GEORGE HARRISON

WHEN I'M SIXTY-FOUR

VIOLINS

Words and Music by JOHN LENNON
and PAUL McCARTNEY

YELLOW SUBMARINE

VIOLINS

Words and Music by JOHN LENNON
and PAUL McCARTNEY

YESTERDAY

VIOLINS

Words and Music by JOHN LENNON
and PAUL McCARTNEY